The Empress's balcony was furnished with wicker furniture, carpets, curtains and decorated with a variety of plants and fragrant flowers, making a perfect refuge for rest and relaxation.

THE EMPRESS'S BALCONY
in the Alexander Palace

PAUL GILBERT

PUBLISHED PRIVATELY
2023

THE EMPRESS'S BALCONY
in the Alexander Palace

ISBN: 9798396043374

Researched and written
by
Paul Gilbert
Founder and Administrator
of
Nicholas II. Emperor. Tsar. Saint.
Web sites & Facebook pages

E-mail:
royalrussia@yahoo.com

Blog:
tsarnicholas.org

COPYRIGHT © 2023
ALL RIGHTS RESERVED

COPYRIGHT NOTICE

All rights reserved under international copyright conventions.

No part of this book may be reproduced or utilized in any manner in any form or by any means, whatsoever, including electronic or mechanical, photocopying, recording, or by any information storage and retrieval system, without written permission except in the case of brief quotations embodied in critical articles and reviews.

This book is sold subject to the condition that it shall not, by way of trade or otherwise, be lent, re-sold, hired out, or otherwise circulated without the author's prior consent in any form of binding or cover other than in which it is published and without a similar condition including this condition imposed on the subsequent purchaser.

COVER PHOTO

Empress Alexandra Feodorovna relaxing on the balcony of the Alexander Palace, Tsarskoye Selo

I must apologize for the quality of some of the photographs, however, this is something which I have no control over. Where possible, photographs have been chosen for their visual impact, but historical accuracy has made it vital to include a number of photographs whose quality is poor, but whose value as historical documents is considerable. Sadly, during the Soviet years, many photographs of the Imperial family were stored under poor conditions and their standard is low.

I have made every effort to include the year each photograph was taken, based on resources made available to me, however, many are also noticeably absent from their respective captions.

Empress Alexandra Feodorovna. 1911

**List of members of the Russian Imperial Family,
their relatives and friends featured in this pictorial**

Empress Alexandra Feodorovna (1872-1918)

Emperor Nicholas II (1868-1918)

Grand Duchess Olga Nikolaevna (1895-1918)

Grand Duchess Tatiana Nikolaevna (1897-1918)

Grand Duchess Maria Nikolaevna (1899-1918)

Grand Duchess Anastasia Nikolaevna (1901-1918)

Tsesarevich Alexei Nikolaevich (1904-1918)

Dowager Empress Maria Feodorovna (1847-1928)

Grand Duchess Olga Alexandrovna (1882-1960)

Duke Peter Alexandrovich of Oldenburg (1868-1924)

Grand Duke Mikhail Alexandrovich (1878-1918)

Grand Duchess Elizabeth Feodorovna (1864-1918)

Anna Alexandrovna Taneeva-Vyrubova (1884-1964)

View of Empress Alexandra Feodorovna's balcony in the Alexander Palace. 1904

Introduction

In 1896, Emperor Nicholas II personally appointed Silvio Amvrosievich Danini (1867-1942) architect of the Tsarskoye Selo Palace Administration, and on 5th October 1911, he was awarded the title of Chief Architect of the Imperial Court.

Danini was responsible for the construction of more than 40 buildings in Tsarskoye Selo [renamed Pushkin in 1937] – many of which have survived to the present day.

He is probably best known for his development of the Alexander Palace – which served as the preferred residence of Nicholas II and his family, from 1905 to 1917.

Between 1896-1898 – Danini carried out the reconstruction of the eastern [left] wing of the Alexander Palace, which included the personal apartments of Nicholas II and Alexandra Feodorovna. In addition, he ordered the construction of an underground passageway between the palace and the Palace Kitchen.

In 1896, Danini installed the famous L-shaped iron balcony for the Empress, which was accessed via the Maple Drawing Room.

The History and Restoration of the Maple Drawing Room in the Alexander Palace

The Maple Drawing Room in the Alexander Palace is a vivid example of the Russian Art Nouveau Style. This interior, as well as the New Study of Nicholas II and the children's rooms on the second floor, was created on the site of the former Concert Hall, built according to the design of Giacomo Quarenghi (1744-1817), which had not been used for its intended purpose for many years.

The decoration of the interior was carried out by the Meltzer brothers' firm in 1902–1904. The walls were painted a warm pink colour and decorated with mouldings of rose stems, foliage and flowers unfolding along the upper walls and ceiling.

Roman Meltzer proposed an original solution for lighting the Maple Drawing Room: along the perimeter of the room, separating the walls from the ceiling plafond, there was a large cornice that masked about two hundred electrical lamps.

A mezzanine was installed which connected the room to the Emperor's New Study. Its decoration was a "Tiffany style" mantel mirror in a metal frame with multi-coloured glass inserts featuring stylized roses.

The interior had several cozy corners where the Empress could do needlework, reading and painting. The children often played or did their homework in this room, the family often joined the Empress in this room at five o'clock for tea.

The huge windows of the room were hung in rich Darmstadt fabrics and delicate lace curtains.

The Maple Drawing Room was decorated with a showcase, the walls and a door made of mirrored glass. It contained Faberge's Imperial Easter Eggs from the collection of Alexandra Feodorovna, as well as Italian Venetian glass vases.

The drawing room was always decorated with fresh flowers: tropical plants and palms were placed in tubs, cut flowers of different varieties from the garden and nursery were placed in vases year-round.

The interior decoration was significantly damaged during the Great Patriotic War (1941-45). In the post-war period, during the adaptation of the palace as the Pushkin Museum, some of the surviving elements of the Maple Drawing Room – including parts of the mezzanine and wall mouldings – were destroyed as objects of "no value".

Between 2015-2021, the reconstruction and restoration of 15 interiors in the Alexander Palace was carried out, including the Maple Drawing Room.

Researchers, architects, designers and restorers carried out a large and complex work to recreate the stucco decoration of the room's historic interior, including the carved mezzanine and built-in maple furniture, returning the interior to its original appearance.

The stucco decoration was recreated from surviving colour autochromes, vintage photographs and rare analogs, for example, the preserved decoration in the mansion of Heinrich Gilse van der Pals on Angliysky Prospekt in St. Petersburg, where the same decorative technique was used.

The mezzanine which originally connected the Maple Drawing Room to the Emperor's New Study had been sealed off when the Alexander Palace reopened as a museum in the 1990s. During the current restoration process, when the walls were opened which connected the two rooms, a small fragment of the original decoration of the Maple Drawing Room was discovered, which assisted experts with regard to the original shade of pink and the design of the rose-stucco reliefs used in the original interior.

Pre-Revolution view of Empress Alexandra Feodorovna's balcony in the Alexander Palace

View of Empress Alexandra Feodorovna's balcony in the Alexander Palace in 1938

Pre-WWII view of Empress Alexandra Feodorovna's balcony in the Alexander Palace

20th century postcard depicting the Alexander Palace and the Empress's balcony, situated in the eastern wing of the palace. The balcony was sheltered from the elements with awnings and drapes, which allowed the Empress and her family to use it year round.

The Empress's Balcony
In the Alexander Palace

The Alexander Palace had three balconies, however, it was the large L-shaped balcony located on the northwest corner of the eastern wing of the palace which is the most famous and the subject of this book - see Danini's plan on page 15.

The second balcony was located on the corner of the western wing of the palace, adjacent to the Palace Chapel, while the third rotunda-shaped balcony was located on the corner of the western wing of palace, adjacent to the Blue Drawing Room. Each of the three balconies featured a walkway which led into the garden and adjacent park - see plans on pages 13 and 14.

In 1896, Silvio Danini installed a large iron balcony for the personal use of Empress Alexandra Feodorovna and her family. The balcony was accessed via the Maple Drawing Room and extended down to the corner of the eastern wing - see plans on pages 13 and 14. A large French door lead out onto the balcony.

The balcony was a favourite place for the Empress and her family year-round, even in winter. Meals and teas were often served here on tables laiden with masses of fragrant flowers on fine tablecloths with china, silver and crystal. Hand-inscribed menus on heavily engraved stock with Imperial double-eagles were placed at each setting. Heavy curtains decorated with a Greek fret pattern were hung between the columns of the balcony to provide protection from sun or bad weather.

The balcony was completely wired for electricity during the First World War, in 1915, so that the family could remain here at night. The wicker furniture often used on the balcony was made by injured soldiers.

In addition, the balcony was decorated with a variety of plants and fragrant flowers, making a perfect refuge for rest and relaxation.

The Empress's balcony became a favourite setting for taking family photographs, taken by the Empress and her children, all of whom were avid amateur photographers. More than a century later, these iconic images provide us with a rare glimpse into the private lives of the Imperial Family.

In the spring of 1946, the Leningrad Executive Committee issued an order for the transfer of the Alexander Palace and the Lyceum to the Institute of Russian Literature of the USSR Academy of Sci-

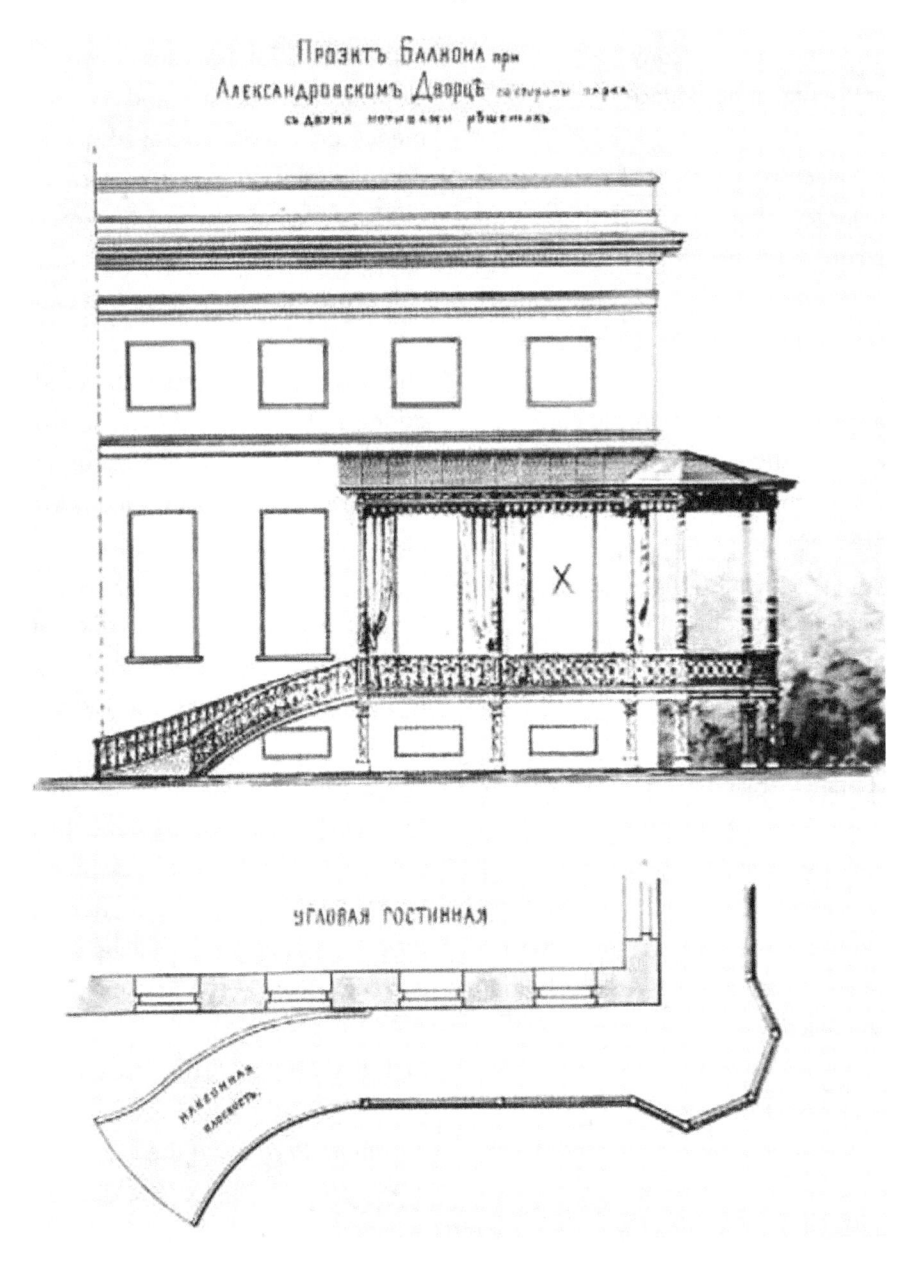

Danini's plan for Empress Alexandra Feodorovna's balcony

ences. This provided the palace with some degree of protection from being abandoned or demolished.

In order to give an adequate assessment of the design solutions implemented in 1947–1949 during the adaptation of the palace to the needs of the institute, it was necessary to consider the works in the Alexander Palace as part of the grandiose project of the Pushkin House to create a scientific town in Pushkin dedicated to the history of Russian literature.

The Lyceum (which then became a museum), Kitaeva's dacha, the houses of Tepper de Fergusson [later Anna Vyrubova's home] and E.A. Engelhardt and several other buildings used as apartments for employees were also transferred to the jurisdiction of the Academy of Sciences.

The Alexander Palace thus became a literary museum and a repository of the priceless manuscript collection of the Pushkin House. The project, developed by architect L.M. Bezverkhny, proceeded from these goals. The remnants of the decoration of the late 19th - early 20th centuries were eliminated and replaced by stylized classical elements, conceived as the return of an authentic spirit to the creation of Quarenghi. The balcony, arranged in the 1890s by S.A. Danini, was dismantled, the door leading onto the balcony was removed, new doorways were made in the living quarters of Alexandra Feodorovna. The Maple Living Room was divided into two rooms.

Despite the extensive restoration work carried out in the eastern wing of the Alexander Palace between 2015-21, the recreation of the balcony was not part of the overall plan.

The Tsarskoye Selo State Museum decided that the balcony is not going to be restored because they wanted to preserve the purity of Giacomo Quarenghi's Neoclassical masterpiece.

Some may consider this an odd decision, especially given that the administration made the decision to reconstruct the late 19th-early 20th century interiors.

Having said that, let us hope that if funding should be made possible, that the palace administration will consider such a project for the future.

In the meantime, we have to content ourselves with the selection of vintage photographs which have survived to this day, and are presented in this pictorial.

Plan of the Alexander Palace which shows the locations of each of the balconies

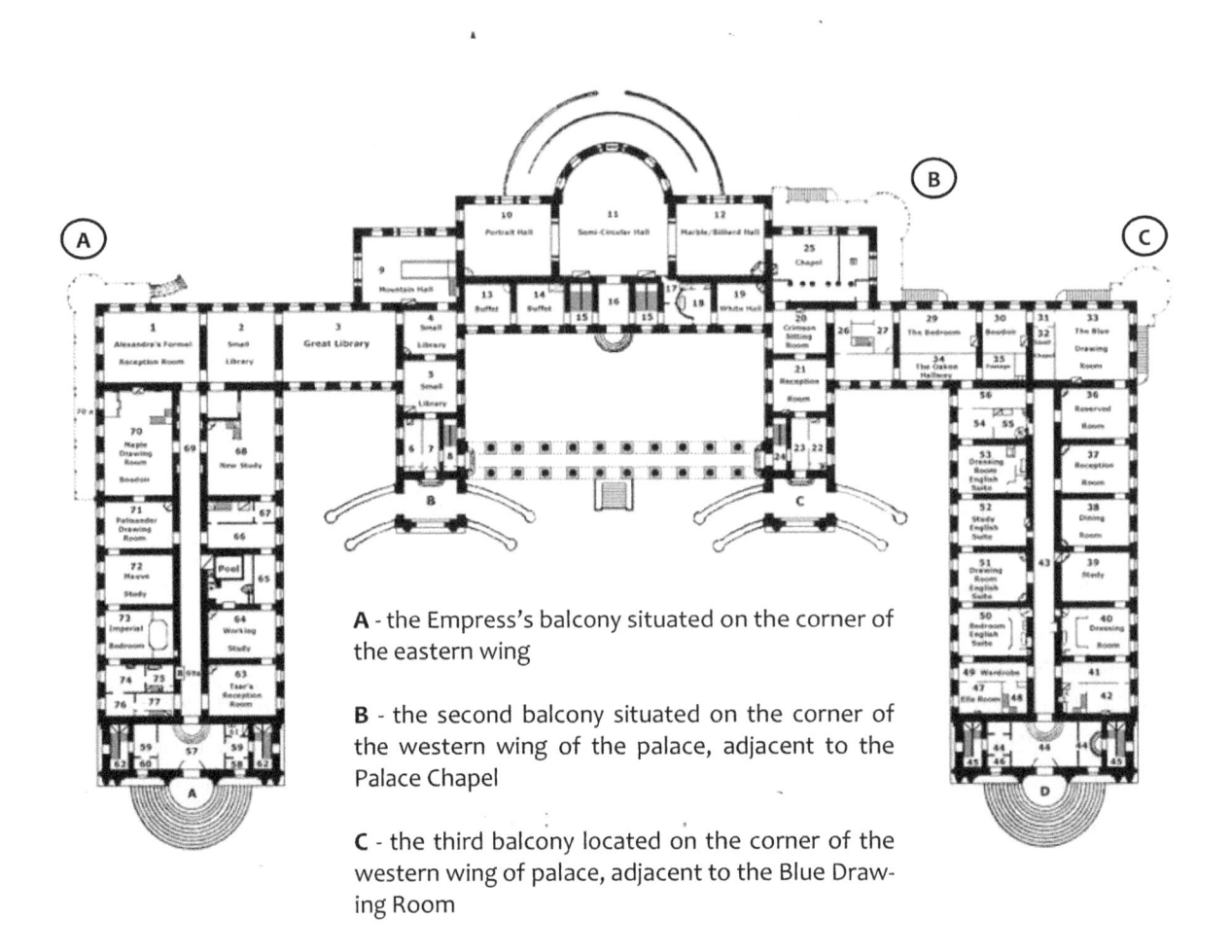

A - the Empress's balcony situated on the corner of the eastern wing

B - the second balcony situated on the corner of the western wing of the palace, adjacent to the Palace Chapel

C - the third balcony located on the corner of the western wing of palace, adjacent to the Blue Drawing Room

Detailed plan of the eastern wing which shows the location of the Empress's balcony (70a)

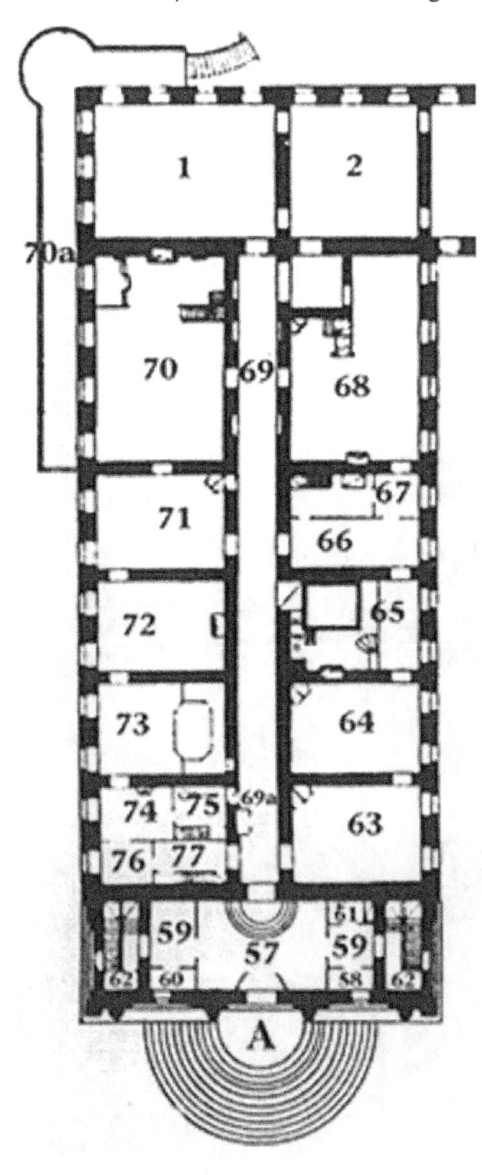

1. Alexandra's Formal Reception Room
2. Small Library
70. Maple Room
70a. Balcony
71. Pallisander Room
72. Mauve Room
73. Imperial Bedroom
74. Dressing Room
75. Toilet
76. Passage
77. Aide d'camp's Room
A. Imperial Entrance
57. Vestibule
63. Tsar's Reception Room
64. Working Study
65. Tsar's Bathroom
66. Nicholas's Dressing Room
67. Valet's Room
68. New Study
69. Corridor
69a. Elevator

Empress Alexandra Feodorovna and Emperor Nicholas II

Empress Alexandra Feodorovna and Emperor Nicholas II

Emperor Nicholas II. 1907

Emperor Nicholas II. 1907

Emperor Nicholas II. 1907

Emperor Nicholas II

Emperor Nicholas II

Emperor Nicholas II. 1916

Emperor Nicholas II. 1915

Emperor Nicholas II. 1915

Emperor Nicholas II. 1915

Emperor Nicholas II. 1915

Emperor Nicholas II. 1915

Emperor Nicholas II. 1915

Emperor Nicholas II. 1915

Emperor Nicholas II. 1915

Emperor Nicholas II. 1915

Emperor Nicholas II with his mother the Dowager Empress Maria Feodorovna. 1915

Emperor Nicholas II and Empress Alexandra Feodorovna

Grand Duke Mikhail Alexandrovich, Duke Peter Alexandrovich of Oldenburg, Grand Duchess Olga Alexandrovna, Emperor Nicholas II with Dowager Empress Marie Feodorovna with her back to the camera

Emperor Nicholas II and Grand Duchess Tatiana Nikolaevna. 1906

Emperor Nicholas II and Grand Duchess Tatiana Nikolaevna

Empress Alexandra Feodorovna

Empress Alexandra Feodorovna

Empress Alexandra Feodorovna

Empress Alexandra Feodorovna

Empress Alexandra Feodorovna

Empress Alexandra Feodorovna

Empress Alexandra Feodorovna

Empress Alexandra Feodorovna

Empress Alexandra Feodorovna

Empress Alexandra Feodorovna

Empress Alexandra Feodorovna

Empress Alexandra Feodorovna

Empress Alexandra Feodorovna

Empress Alexandra Feodorovna

Empress Alexandra Feodorovna. Winter 1909-10

Empress Alexandra Feodorovna. Winter 1909-10

Empress Alexandra Feodorovna. Winter 1909-10

Empress Alexandra Feodorovna. Winter 1909-10

Empress Alexandra Feodorovna

Anna Alexandrovna Taneeva-Vyrubova

Anna Alexandrovna Taneeva-Vyrubova with Empress Alexandra Feodorovna

Empress Alexandra Feodorovna. 1912

Grand Duchess Olga Alexandrovna (second from right) with her nieces Anastasia, Tatiana and Olga

Nicholas II, Grand Duchesses Olga, Tatiana, Maria, Anastasia, and Tsesarevich Alexei. 1910

Nicholas II, Tsesarevich Alexei Nikolaevich, Alexandra Feodorovna and Grand Duchess Olga Nikolaevna

OTMAA: Olga, Tatiana, Maria, Anastasia and Alexei

from left to right (back row): Grand Duchesses Maria, Olga, Tatiana, Grand Duke Michael Alexandrovich
from left to right (front row): Grand Duchess Anastasia, Emperor Nicholas II, Tsesarevich Alexei

Grand Duchesses Olga and Tatiana Nikolaevna with Emperor Nicholas II

Empress Alexandra with her daughters Anastasia, Tatiana and Maria. 1905

Grand Duchesses Anastasia, Maria, Tatiana and Olga Nikolaevna. 1905

Empress Alexandra Feodorovna with her children

Empress Alexandra Feodorovna with her children

Empress Alexandra Feodorovna with Tsesarevich Alexei Nikolaevich

Grand Duchesses Tatiana and Olga Nikolaevna

Grand Duchesses Anastasia and Maria Nikolaevna. 1910

Grand Duchess Anastasia Nikolaevna. 1905

OTMAA: Tatiana, Olga, Anastasia, Maria and Alexei

Grand Duchesses Maria, Tatiana, Olga and Anastasia Nikolaevna

Grand Duchesses Olga and Maria Nikolaevna. 1912

Grand Duchesses Olga and Tatiana Nikolaevna. 1912

Grand Duchess Tatiana Nikolaevna. 1912

Grand Duchess Tatiana Nikolaevna. 1912

Grand Duchess Olga Nikolaevna. 1906

Grand Duchess Tatiana Nikolaevna. 1906

Grand Duchess Maria Nikolaevna. 1906

Grand Duchess Anastasia Nikolaevna. 1906

Grand Duchess Olga Nikolaevna

Grand Duchess Tatiana Nikolaevna. 1911

Grand Duchess Tatiana Nikolaevna

Grand Duchess Anastasia Nikolaevna. 1915

Grand Duchess Anastasia Nikolaevna

Grand Duchesses Maria, Olga and Tatiana Nikolaevna. 1916

Grand Duchess Olga Nikolaevna. 1916

Grand Duchess Tatiana Nikolaevna. 1916

Grand Duchess Maria Nikolaevna. 1916

Grand Duchess Anastasia Nikolaevna. 1916

Emperor Nicholas II with his son and heir Tsesarevich Alexei Nikolaevich

Emperor Nicholas II with his son and heir Tsesarevich Alexei Nikolaevich

Emperor Nicholas II with his son and heir Tsesarevich Alexei Nikolaevich

Emperor Nicholas II with his son and heir Tsesarevich Alexei Nikolaevich

Tsesarevich Alexei Nikolaevich

Tsesarevich Alexei Nikolaevich

Grand Duchess Elizabeth Feodorovna

Grand Duchess Elizabeth Feodorovna

Grand Duke Mikhail Alexandrovich

Grand Duke Mikhail Alexandrovich

THE EMPRESS'S CHAIR
in the Alexander Palace
PAUL GILBERT

Paperback edition. 120 pages. 106 black-and-white photographs

AVAILABLE FROM AMAZON

NICHOLAS II

EMPEROR · TSAR · SAINT

Dedicated to clearing the name of Russia's much slandered Tsar

tsarnicholas.org

Made in the USA
Las Vegas, NV
25 March 2025